THE HYMN OF JESUS

According to G. R. S. Mead, the translator of this beautiful Hymn of Jesus, there is strong reason to presume that this work is a very early Christian mystery ritual—perhaps the oldest Christian ritual preserved to us.

G. R. S. Mead was a renowned British scholar and a recognized authority on Christian origins and Gnostic and Hermetic literature. He died in 1933, but his works are still widely read. In his commentary on this hymn in ritual form he has offered an interpretation of its inner, spiritual meaning.

THE HYMN OF JESUS

Echoes from the Gnosis

Translated with comments
by
G. R. S. MEAD

A QUEST BOOK

Miniature

Published under a grant from The Kern Foundation

THE THEOSOPHICAL PUBLISHING HOUSE
Wheaton, Ill., U.S.A.
Madras, India — London, England

First published in 1907 by The Theosophical
  Publishing Society, London and Benares

Second impression 1963 published by
  John M. Watkins, London

Quest Book edition (first U.S. edition) 1973 published by The Theosophical Publishing House,
  Wheaton, Illinois, a department of The Theosophical Society in America, by arrangement with
  John M. Watkins, London

ISBN: 0-8356-0432-2

Printed in the United States of America

CONTENTS

THE HYMN OF JESUS.

PREAMBLE.

Just as many other settings of the Sayings and Doings of the Lord existed prior to and alongside of the canonical Gospels, so were there, prior to and alongside of the subsequently selected or canonical Acts, many other narratives professing to record the doings and sayings of the Apostles and Disciples of the Lord.

Most of these originated in circles which were subsequently called heretical, and many of them were later on worked over by orthodox editors to suit doctrinal preconceptions, and so preserved for the edification of large numbers in the Catholic or General Church.

As Lipsius says : " Almost every fresh

1

editor of such narratives, using that free-
dom which all antiquity was wont to
allow itself in dealing with literary monu-
ments, would recast the materials which
lay before him, excluding whatever might
not suit his theological point of view—
dogmatic statements, for example,
speeches, prayers, etc., for which he
would substitute other formulæ of his
own composition, and further expanding
and abridging after his own pleasure, or
as the immediate object which he had in
view might dictate."

Some of these edited and re-edited
documents, though for the most part they
have come down to us in a very fragmen-
tary condition, still preserve distinct
traces of their Gnostic origin ; and
Lipsius has shown that their Gnosticism
is not to be ascribed to third century
Manichæism, as had been previously
assumed by many, but to the general
Gnosis of the second century.

There was a very wide circulation of
such religious romances in the second

century, for they formed the main means of Gnostic public propaganda.

The technical inner teachings of Gnosticism were assailed by the subsequently orthodox Church Fathers with misrepresentation and overwhelmed with ridicule.

To these onslaughts the Gnostics, as far as we are aware, made no reply ; most probably because they were bound by oaths of secrecy on the one hand, and on the other knew well that the mysteries of the inner life could not be decided by vulgar debate.

The mystic teachings of their Gospel were for those who knew the nature of the inner life by direct experience ; for the rest they were foolishness.

Their Acts-romances also appear often to be based on actual occurrences of the inner life and on direct spiritual experience, subsequently worked up into popular forms ; the marvellous complexity and baffling sublimity of apocalyptic ecstasy, and the over-abundant and pregnant technology which delighted the members of the inner circles of the Gnostic Christians, were excluded, and all was reduced to simpler terms.

These marvellous narratives may seem vastly fantastic to the modern mind, but to every shade of Christianity in those days, they were entirely credible. The orthodox did not repudiate the marvellous nature of the narratives; what they opposed with such bitterness was the doctrinal implications with which they were involved.

These Acts-romances thus formed the intermediate link between the General Church and the inner teachings of Gnosticism, and they were so popular that they could not be disposed of by ridicule simply. Another method had to be used.

To quote from Lipsius again: "Catholic bishops and teachers knew not how better to stem this flood of Gnostic writings and their influence among the faithful, than by boldly adopting the most popular narratives from the heretical books, and, after carefully eliminating the poison of false doctrine, replacing them in this purified form in the hands of the public."

Fortunately for some of us, this " purification " has not been complete, and some of the " poison of false doctrine " has thus been preserved. Among other things of great beauty for which we are grateful, we especially thank a kindly providence for the preservation of the Hymn of Jesus.

The earliest collection of these Gnostic Acts is said to have been made by a certain Leucius, surnamed Charinus. There is a tradition, though of somewhat doubtful authenticity, that this Leucius was a disciple of John. If we accept it at all, this John must be taken for the writer of the Fourth Gospel, and not the John of the original Twelve.

It would be impossible here to enter into any discussion of the baffling Johannine problem ; those of our readers, however, who are interested in the manifest Gnostic implications with which this

problem is involved as far as it relates to
the Fourth Gospel, should read Kreyenbühl's exhaustive and instructive study
Das Evangelium der Wahrheit (Berlin ;
1900, 1905). His " new solution of the
Johannine question," which Kreyenbühl
entitles " The Gospel of the Truth,"
boldly claims an immediate Gnostic origin
for the Fourth Gospel; and this courageous
pioneer of a new way even goes so far as
to contend that the writer of what is
indubitably the most spiritual of all the
Gospels, was no other than Mænander,
the teacher of Basilides. It is instructive
to remark that this voluminous and important work has been passed over with
complete silence in this country.

At any rate the Leucian Acts were
early ; in the opinion of Zahn this collection was made at a time when the Gnostics
were not yet considered heretical, that is
to say prior to 150 A.D.—say 130 A.D.

Lipsius on the other hand places them
in the second half of the second century,
towards the end, and so does Hennecke.

6

This maximum of date they are compelled to concede, because Clement of Alexandria at the end of the second century quotes from the Gnostic *Acts of John* which indubitably formed part of the Leucian collection.

The controversy between Lipsius and Zahn was conditioned by the fact that they both agreed that the *Acts of John* quote from the Fourth Gospel. Zahn placed this Gospel earlier in date than Lipsius and was anxious to find in the Acts an early witness to that Gospel, indeed the earliest witness.

It has, however, been strongly contested by Corssen whether the Acts quote from the Gospel ; and as far as I can myself see from the passages adduced, there does not seem to be absolute evidence of any *direct* quotation. There is indubitably a close similarity of diction, as is so often the case in similar problems concerning nearly contemporary documents ; but the problem is more easily satisfied by considering the writers as belonging to the

same circle, than by seeking to prove
direct literary plagiarism.

However this may be, we are not to
suppose that Leucius *invented* the Acts ;
he collected and adapted and wrote up
the material. If he had invented all of
it, he would have been a genius of no
mean order.

Leucius has a style of his own, and he
also moved in a certain sweet atmosphere
that is characteristic of the best in the
Johannine tradition—the tradition of love,
and intimacy, and simplicity ; very different, for instance, from the more formal
Pauline atmosphere.

The *Acts of John* are indubitably
Leucian, and judging by literary style so
are the *Acts of Peter*. As to the rest of
the *Acts* of the original Leucian collection,
there is at present no certainty, and those
assigned to Leucius by later writers must
be put on one side as far as their present
remains are concerned.

It has been surmised by James that as
Luke (Loukas) wrote the Orthodox Acts,

the writer who wrote the Gnostic Acts
called himself Leucius (Leukios) to suggest
he was one and the same person ; but
this I consider highly improbable. The
Gnostics are in general inventors and not
copyists.

It is also of interest to note that Zahn
considers that the account of the genesis
of the Fourth Gospel given by the writer
of the Muratorian Fragment (c. 170 A.D.)
was taken from the Leucian Acts. This
Gospel is there said to have been written
by a certain John, who was " of the
Disciples." His " fellow-disciples and
bishops " had apparently urged him to
write a Gospel, but John hesitated to
accept the responsibility, and proposed
that they should all fast together for
three days, and tell one another if any-
thing was revealed to them. On the same
night it is revealed to Andrew, who is
" of the Apostles," that while all revised
John should write down all things in his
own name.

If this information is taken from the

Leucian Acts, it follows of course that
their writer was acquainted with the
Fourth Gospel. If we take this as certain
—though from the adduced parallel
phrases alone I cannot myself be quite
certain—then the question arises how
could Leucius have put into the mouth of
John doctrines which are opposed to the
teaching of the Gospel ? To this question
James gives the following answer :

" His notion is that St. John wrote for
the multitude certain comparatively plain
and easy episodes in the life of the Lord :
but that to the inner circle of the faithful
his teaching was widely different. In
the Gospel and Epistles we have his exo-
teric teaching : in the Acts his esoteric."

This of course exactly reverses the
relation that Corssen supposes to have
existed between the Acts and Gospel ;
namely that the author of the Acts did
not know the Gospel at all.

It is of course the general Gnostic
position that all true scripture had an
under-meaning. The gospel-narratives

were written for the people, but at the same time in such a fashion as to set forth allegorically the mysteries.

If, then, any propaganda of these hidden mysteries was to be attempted in a less veiled form, it follows that a more spiritual standpoint had to be insisted on ; and the popular narrative which was generally taken in a physical and material sense, was replaced by a more plastic and suggestive setting and exposition.

But—we may ask, at any rate in the case of the Fourth Gospel—was it the Gospel-narrative that was prior in date, and the Gnostic re-writing of Gospel-incidents subsequent ; or was it that the Gnostic ideas existed prior to the writing of the Gospel, and the matter incorporated into the Gnostic Acts derived directly from the same body of ideas that inspired the Gospel ?

As it is now proved beyond all question that the Gnosis was pre-Christian, and that in what is generally called Gnosticism we are dealing with a Christianized

Gnosis which demonstrably existed in the time of Paul, and which Paul found already existing in the Churches, we must conclude that there is nothing inherently improbable in the latter alternative.

Moreover, the Gnosticism of the *Acts of John* is general and simple and cannot be assigned to this or that particular school of the Christian Gnosis.

The marvellous and beautiful Hymn, which is the subject of this small volume, is found in what are without doubt the Leucian *Acts of John*. That, however, Leucius himself composed the Hymn is by no means to be taken for granted. Leucius was a collector and redactor—he used sources ; and I have myself no doubt that the Hymn existed in Gnostic circles prior to the composition of the *Acts*—indeed, that it was a most precious document.

The first external testimony to our Hymn is found in its use by the Priscillianists, in Spain, in the last third of the fourth century. The great movement known under the name of Priscillianism was a powerful revival of Gnosticism and Oriental mysticism and theosophy which poured over the Peninsula.

The views of the Priscillianists on scripture were those of the rest of the Gnostics in general ; their canon was catholic in the widest meaning of the term. Just as the Jewish scriptures were an imperfect revelation as compared with the general Christian books, so were the popular scriptures of Christianity imperfect in comparison with the revelations of the Gnosis.

As the Old Covenant books were considered to be replete with types and figures, images and shadows of the Gospel-teaching, so were the books of the New Testament, in their turn, held to be figurative and symbolical of the inner teachings of the Gnosis. The former were intended for those of Faith, the latter for those in Gnosis.

Against this view Augustine and Jerome

13

waged remorseless war ; for the country was flooded with an immense number of Gnostic documents. The Priscillianists were persecuted and martyred and the main care of the orthodox bishops was to seize their books and destroy them.

Ceretius, one of the bishops presumably, had sent Augustine some of the books of these Gnostics ; he himself seems to have been inclined to approve them. Augustine, in his answer, picks out for detailed criticism one document only—our Hymn. Concerning this he writes :

" As for the Hymn which they say is that of our Lord Jesus Christ, and which has so greatly aroused your veneration, it is usually found in apocryphal writings, not peculiar to the Priscillianists but used by other heretics."

Augustine adds a quotation, from the introduction of the Gnostic M.S. of the Hymn, which runs :

14

THE HYMN OF JESUS

"The Hymn of the Lord which He sang in secret to the holy Apostles, His disciples, for it is said in the Gospel: 'And after singing a hymn He ascended the mount.' This Hymn is not put in the canon, because of those who think according to themselves, and not according to the Spirit and Truth of God, and that it is written: 'It is good to hide the sacrament of the King; but it is honourable to reveal the works of God.'"

The Gospel referred to cannot be either Matthew (xxvi. 31) or Mark (xiv. 26), both of which read: "And after singing a hymn *they went out* to the Mount of Olives." The second quotation I am unable to trace.

An important point which will concern us later on is that Ceretius found the Hymn by itself and not in its context in the *Acts*; it was in all probability extracted for liturgical purposes.

It is, moreover, evident from what Augustine writes in the first passage we have quoted that the Hymn was well-known in Gnostic circles.

It would also seem as though Augustine, who wrote in Latin, was dealing with a Latin translation, rather than that he translated the quotation himself in his answer to Ceretius.

Part only of the Greek text of this famous Hymn was known prior to 1899, when James published a hitherto unknown and very important fragment of the *Acts of John*, found in a fourteenth century M.S., in the Vienna Imperial Library. This contained what seems to be the full text of our Hymn, though, unfortunately, copied by a sometimes very careless scribe. Nearly the whole of this lengthy fragment consists of a monologue put into the mouth of John, and in it we have preserved to us a very remarkable tradition of the Gnostic side of the life of the Master; or, if it be preferred, of incidents in the "occult" life of Jesus.

The whole setting of the christology is what is called "docetic." Our fragment is thus a most valuable addition to our knowledge of Docetism, and at last gives us a satisfactory reason why this view was held so widely by the Gnostics. Indeed it is now the most important source we possess, and puts the whole question on a different footing. In future our fragment must always be taken first as the *locus classicus* in any discussion of the question.

Docetism was a theory which found its confirmation in narratives and legends of certain psychic or spiritual powers ascribed to the " perfect man."

The christological and soteriological theories of the Gnostic philosophers were not, as many would have us believe, invented altogether *à priori* ; they rested, I hold, on the basis of a veritable historical fact, which has for the most part been obscured out of all recognition by the flood of physical objective historicizing narratives of the origins.

After His death, I believe, as many a Gnostic tradition claims, the Christ did

17

return and teach His disciples and true lovers in the inner circles, and this fact which was made known to their consciousness in many marvellous ways, was to a large extent the origin of the protean Gnostic tradition of an inner instruction.

He returned in the only way He could return in *this way* of return—namely, in a subtle or " spiritual " mode or " body." This " body " could be made visible at will, could even be made sensible to touch, but was, compared with the normally objective physical body, an " illusory " body—hence the term " docetic."

But just as the external tradition of those who are considered the original Jewish Christians, the Ebionîm (or Poor), was gradually transmuted and sublimated, so that it, finally, exalted Jesus from the status of a simple prophet in which it originally regarded him, unto the full Power and Glory of Godhead itself ; so the internal tradition extended the doubtlessly simple original docetic notion to every department of the huge soteriological structure raised by Gnostic genius.

The Leucian *Acts of John* pertain to the latter stream of tendencies, and " John " is the personification, so to say, of one of the lines of tradition of that protean Docetism, which had its origin in one of the best-known and most important facts of the spiritual life, or of " occult " experience, and of those marvellous teachings of initiation which became subsequently historicized or woven into historic settings, and which " John " in our fragment, sums up in the words :

" I held firmly this one thing in myself, that the Lord contrived all things symbolically and by a dispensation towards men, for their conversion and salvation."

That is to say, that all truly inspired narratives of the Doings and Sayings of the Christ are typical ; or again, that He who is Christ, in all He does and says, as Christ, acts with the Cosmic Order. This

is His " economy " and " ministry "—
the doing of His " Father's business."

We will now turn to the Hymn itself,
and first give a version of it from Bonnet's
text. In the newly-recovered fragment it
is introduced as follows :

" Now before He was taken by the
lawless Jews—by them who are under
the law of the lawless Serpent—He
gathered us together and said :

" ' Before I am delivered over unto
them we will hymn the Father, and so
go forth to what lieth before [us].'

" Then bidding us make as it were a
ring, by holding each others' hands, with
Him in the midst, He said :

" ' Answer " Amen " to Me.'

" Then He began to hymn a hymn and
say :

THE HYMN OF JESUS

THE HYMN.

Glory to Thee, Father !

(And we going round in a ring answered to Him :)

Amen !

Glory to Thee, Word (*Logos*) !

Amen !

Glory to Thee, Grace (*Charis*) !

Amen !

Glory to Thee, Spirit !
Glory to Thee, Holy One !
Glory to Thy Glory !

Amen !

THE HYMN OF JESUS

We praise Thee, O Father;
We give Thanks to Thee, O Light;
In Whom Darkness dwells not!

Amen!

(For what we give thanks to the Logos).

[Or, if we adopt the " emended " text:
For what we give thanks, I say:]

I would be saved; and I would save.

Amen!

I would be loosed; and I would loose.

Amen!

I would be wounded; and I would
wound.

[Or, I would be pierced; and I would
pierce.

22

Another reading has :
I would be dissolved (or consumed for love) ; and I would dissolve.]

Amen !

I would be begotten ; and I would beget.

Amen !

I would eat ; and I would be eaten

Amen !

I would hear ; and I would be heard.

Amen !

[I would understand ; and] I would be understood ; being all Understanding (*Nous*).

[The first clause I have supplied ; the last is probably a gloss.]

I would be washed; and I would wash.

Amen !

(Grace leadeth the dance.)

I would pipe; dance ye all.

Amen !

I would play a dirge; lament ye all.

Amen !

The one Eight (Ogdoad) sounds (or plays) with us.

Amen !

The Twelfth Number above leadeth the dance.

Amen !

THE HYMN OF JESUS

All whose nature is to dance [doth dance].

Amen !

Who danceth not, knows not what is being done.

Amen !

I would flee ; and I would stay.

Amen !

I would be adorned ; and I would adorn.

[The clauses are reversed in the text.]

Amen !

I would be at-oned ; and I would at-one.

Amen !

I have no dwelling ; and I have dwellings.

Amen !

I have no place ; and I have places.

Amen !

I have no temple ; and I have temples.

Amen !

I am a lamp to thee who seest Me.

Amen !

I am a mirror to thee who under-
standest Me.

Amen !

I am a door to thee who knockest at Me.

Amen !

I am a way to thee a wayfarer.

Amen !

Now answer to My dancing !

See thyself in Me who speak ;
And seeing what I do,
Keep silence on My Mysteries.

Understand, by dancing, what I do ;
For thine is the Passion of Man
That I am to suffer.

Thou couldst not at all be conscious
Of what thou dost suffer,
Were I not sent as thy Word by the
Father.
[The last clause may be emended :
I am thy Word ; I was sent by the Father.]

Seeing what I suffer,

Thou sawest Me as suffering;
And seeing, thou didst not stand,
But wast moved wholly,
Moved to be wise.

Thou hast Me for a couch; rest thou
upon Me.

Who I am thou shalt know when I
depart.
What now I am seen to be, that I am
not.
[But what I am] thou shalt see when
thou comest.

If thou hadst known how to suffer,
Thou wouldst have power not to suffer.
Know [then] how to suffer, and thou
hast power not to suffer.

That which thou knowest not, I Myself
will teach thee.

I am thy God, not the Betrayer's.

THE HYMN OF JESUS

I would be kept in time with holy souls.

In Me know thou the Word of Wisdom.

Say thou to Me again :

Glory to Thee, Father !
Glory to Thee, Word !
Glory to Thee, Holy Spirit !

But as for Me, if thou wouldst know
what I was :
In a word I am the Word who did play
[or dance] all things, and was not shamed
at all.
'Twas I who leaped [and danced].

But do thou understand all, and, understanding, say :

Glory to Thee, Father !

Amen !

(And having danced these things with us, Beloved, the Lord went forth. And we, as though beside ourselves, or wakened out of [deep] sleep, fled each our several ways.)

COMMENTS.

To me it seems almost certain, as I argued in the first edition of *Fragments of a Faith Forgotten*, in 1900, that this Hymn is no hymn, but a mystery-ritual, and perhaps the earliest Christian ritual of which we have any trace.

We have a number of such mystery-rituals in the Coptic Gnostic works—in the extract from the "Books of the Saviour" appended to the so-called *Pistis Sophia* document of the Askew Codex, and in the "Two Books of Ieou" of the Bruce Codex.

In a number of passages the Disciples are bidden to "surround" (that is, join hands round) the Master at certain praise-givings and invocations of the Father, who is addressed as: "Father of all Fatherhood, Boundless Light"—just as

THE HYMN OF JESUS

the Father is hymned as Light in the
last three lines of our opening doxology.

The " Second Book of Ieou " ends with
a long praise-giving, in the inner spaces ;
for these highly mystical treatises deal
with the instruction of the Disciples by
the Master out of the body. This praise-
giving begins as follows (Carl Schmidt,
*Gnost. Schrift. . . . aus d. Codex Bruci-
anus*—Leipzig, 1892—pp. 187 ff.) :

" And He spake unto them, the Twelve :
Surround Me all of you !
And they all surrounded Him. He
said unto them :
Answer to Me [Amen], and sing praise
with Me ; and I will praise My Father for
the Emanation of all Treasures.
And He began to sing a hymn, praising
His Father, and saying :
I praise Thee . . . ; for Thou hast
drawn Thyself unto Thyself altogether in
Truth, till Thou hast set free the space of
this Little Idea [? the Cosmos] ; yet hast
Thou not withdrawn Thyself. For what

now is Thy Will, O Unapproachable God ?

Thereon He made His Disciples answer three times : Amen, Amen, Amen ! "

As far as I can discover from the most recent works of reference, " Amen " is considered by scholars to be a pure Hebrew word. It is said to have been originally an adjective signifying " stability," " firmness," " certainty," which subsequently became an interjection, used first of all in conversation, and then restricted to the most solemn form of asseveration ; as, for instance, in oaths, and, in the temple ritual, in the responses of the congregation to the doxologies and solemn utterances of the priests and readers.

According to the Portuguese reading of the vowels it is pronounced Âmēn (the vowels as in Italian). The Greek transliteration is Amēn.

In *Revelation* (iii. 14), Christ is called the Amen : " These things saith the

Amen, the faithful and true Witness."

We are told that in the great synagogue at Alexandria, at the conclusion of the reader's doxology, the attendant signalled with a flag for the congregation to respond Amen.

This use of this sacred utterance was taken over by the Christian churches ; so that we find Jerome writing : " Like unto celestial thunder the Amen re-echoes."

It is well known that Hebrew and Aramaic are exceedingly rich in loan-words from other languages. I have, however, never seen it yet suggested that Amen may be a loan-word. I would now, with all submission to Hebraist specialists, make this suggestion, for Plutarch in his treatise *On Isis and Osiris* writes (ix. 4) :

" Moreover, while the majority think that the proper name of Zeus with the Egyptians is Amoun (which we by a slight change call Ammōn), Manethō, the Sebennyte, considers it His hidden one, and

that His power of hiding is made plain by
the very articulation of the sound.

"Hecatæus of Abdera, however, says
that the Egyptians use this word to one
another also when they call one to them,
for that its sound has got the power of
'calling to.'

"Wherefore when they call to the First
God—who they think is the same for
every man—as unto the Unmanifest and
Hidden, invoking Him to make Him
manifest and plain to them, they say
'Amoun!'"

Ammōn or Amoun is usually trans-
literated directly from the hieroglyphics as
Amen. We thus learn that in Egypt
Amen was a "word of power," indeed the
chief "word of power" in general theurgic
use.

We cannot suppose that Hecatæus, in
his *History of Egypt*, intended us to
understand that the Egyptians shouted it
after one another in the street. It was

rather used as a word of magic, for evoking the *Ka* of a person, or as the chiefest of all invocations to the Invisible Deity.

The exact parallel is to be found to-day in the use of the " Word of Glory " (the Praṇava), Oṁ or Auṁ, in India.

The sacred dancing was common to all great mystery-ceremonies. Here it will be sufficient to quote from what Philo of Alexandria, in the first quarter of our era, tells us, in his famous treatise *On the Contemplative Life*, about the sacred dances of the Therapeuts or " Servants of God." He writes :

" Then the president rising chants a hymn which has been made in God's honour, either a new one which he has composed, or an old one of the ancient poets.

" For they have left behind them many metres and tunes in trimetric epics, processional hymns, libation-odes, altar-chants, stationary choruses, and dance-songs, all admirably measured off in diversified strains.

"And after him the others also, in bands, in proper order, take up the chanting, while the rest listen in deep silence, except when they have to join in the burden and refrains ; for they all, both men and women, join in. . . .

"After the banquet they keep the holy all-night festival. And this is how it is kept :

"They all stand up in a body ; and about the middle of the ceremony they first of all separate into two bands, men in one and women in the other. And a leader is chosen for each, the conductor whose reputation is greatest and the one most suitable for the post.

"They then chant hymns made in God's honour, in many metres and melodies ; sometimes singing in chorus, sometimes one band beating time to the answering chant of the other, now dancing to its music, now inspiring it, at one time in processional hymns, at another in standing songs, turning and returning in the dance.

" Then when each band has feasted [that is, has sung and danced] apart by itself, drinking of God-pleasing nectar, just as in the Bacchic rites men drink the wine unmixed, they join together, and one chorus is formed of the two bands. . .

" So the chorus of men and women Therapeuts . . . , by means of melodies in parts and harmony—the high notes of the women answering to the deep tones of the men—produces a harmonious and most musical symphony. The ideas are of the most beautiful, the expressions of the most beautiful, and the dancers reverent ; while the goal of the ideas, expressions, and dancers is piety.

" Thus drunken unto morning's light with this fair drunkenness, with no head-heaviness or drowsiness, but with eyes and body fresher even than when they came to the banquet, they take their stand at dawn, when, catching sight of the rising sun, they raise their hands to heaven, praying for Sunlight and Truth, and keenness of Spiritual Vision."

And now we will turn to the text of our Hymn, which pertains to a still higher mystery, first of all dealing with the introductory words of the writer of the *Acts*.

The " lawless Jews " refers to those who are " under the law of the lawless Serpent " ; that is to say, those who are under the sway of Generation as contrasted with those who are under the law of Regeneration, of carnal birth as opposed to spiritual birth ; or again, of the Lesser as contrasted with the Greater Mysteries.

As the pre-Christian Greek redactor of the Naassene Document phrases it (*T.G.H.*, i. 162) :

" For He [the Great Man, the Logos, the Serpent of Wisdom] is Ocean—' birth-causing of gods and birth-causing of men '

—flowing and ebbing for ever, now up and now down."

And on this the early Jewish commentator remarks :

" When Ocean flows down, it is the birth-causing of men ; and when He flows up, . . . it is the birth-causing of gods."

And further on he adds :

" This is the Great Jordan, which flowing downwards and preventing the Sons of Israel from going forth out of Egypt, or from the Intercourse Below, was turned back by Jesus [LXX. for Joshua] and made to flow upwards."

This one and the same Serpent was thus either the Agathodaimōn (or Good Spirit) or the Kakodaimōn (or Evil Spirit), according to the will of man. The regenerated or perfected man, the man of

repentance, he who has turned Home-
wards, or has his "face" set Above, whose
will is being at-oned with the Divine Will,
turns the waters of Ocean upwards, and
thus gives birth to himself as a god.

The doxology of our Hymn is triadic—
Father, Son, Mother.

Charis, Grace or Love, is Wisdom, or
God's Good-Will, the Holy Spirit, or
Great Breath ; that is, the Power and
Spouse of Deity.

The order of the triple praise-giving is
then reversed : Mother, Son, Father ; for
Glory is the Great Presence, the Father.

And finally there is a trinity in unity,
Praise being given to the Father as Light ;
the same as the oft-recurring invocation
in the Coptic Gnostic works : " Father of
all Fatherhood, Boundless Light ! "

The doxology being ended, we come to
a striking series of double clauses or
antitheses.   I at once submit that these
were not originally intended to be uttered

by one and the same person On the
contrary they are evidently amœbæan ;
that is, answering as in a dialogue. Nor
were they addressed to the Disciples ;
there was some single person for whom
the whole was intended, and to whom
much of it is addressed.

If, then, we have before us not a hymn,
but the remains of a mystery-ritual, there
must have been two people in the circle.
One of them was the Master, the Initiator.
Who was the other ? Manifestly, the one
to be initiated.

Now the ultimate end of all Gnosis was
the at-one-ment or union of the little man
with the Great Man, of the human soul
with the Divine Soul.

In the great Wisdom-myth, the human
soul was regarded as the " lost sheep,"
the erring and suffering Sophia fallen into
generation, from which she was saved by
the Christ, her true Lord and Spouse.

On the side of the Great Descent we
have the most wonderful attempts made
by the Gnostics to pierce the veil, of the

mysteries of cosmogony—to catch some glimpse of how the Cosmos came into existence, and was fashioned by the creative power of the Logos, the Supernal Christ. This was called the " enformation according to substance "—the " substance " being the Sophia or Wisdom Herself as viewed in Her self-isolation from the Plērōma or Fullness of Divine Being, the Transcendent Presence.

On the way of the Great Ascent or Return, the Gnosis attempted to raise the veil of the mysteries of soteriology, or of the rescue of the separated human soul, and its restoration to the Bosom of the Divine. This was called the " enformation according to gnosis "—that is, Self-consciousness.

The duologue is therefore carried on by those who are acting out the mystery of the Sophia and the Christ ; though we should never forget that they are in reality or essentially one and the same Person, the lower and higher self in the Presence of the Great Self.

The twelve disciples are the representatives of the powers of the Master, sent forth (apostles) into the outer worlds, corresponding with the Great Twelve of the Presence, the Twelve Above; and they dance to the dancing or cosmic motions of the Twelve, even as the candidate, or neophyte, the Sophia below, dances to the cosmic motion of the Charis or Grace or Sophia Above.

And if this rite be duly consummated, the Presence that enwraps the doers of the mystery is Divine. The Presence is that of the Father Himself, who has no human form, but is as it were a " Heart," or " Head," a " Face," a Shekinah or Glory. How the seers of the Gnosis conceived this marvel of the Godhead may perhaps be seized dimly in the following passages from the " Untitled Apocalypse " of the Bruce Codex (*F.F.F.*, p. 548) :

" The Outline of His Face is beyond all possibility of knowing in the Outer Worlds—those Worlds that ever seek His

Face, desiring to know it ; for His Word has gone forth into them, and they long to see Him.

" The Light of His Eyes penetrates the Spaces of the Outer Plērōma ; and the Word that comes forth from His Mouth penetrates the Above and the Below.

" The Hair of His Head is the number of the Hidden Worlds, and the Outline of His Face is the type of the Æons [*i.e.*, Perfect Spheres and Eternities].

" The Hairs of His Face are the number of the Outer Worlds, and the Outspreading of His Hands is the manifestation of the Cross. . . .

" The Source of the Cross is the Man [Logos] whom no man can comprehend.

" He is the Father ; He is the Source from which the Silence [the Mother of the Æons] wells."

And as to the consummation of at-one-ment and the state of him who makes joyful surrender of himself unto the Powers, " and thus becoming Powers he is in God," as Pœmandrēs teaches, some intuition may be gleaned from the same document which tells of the Host of Powers, " having wreaths (or crowns) on their heads "—that is Æons or Christs or Masters crowned with their Twelve Powers, and all the other orderings of spiritual energies (*F.F.F.*, p. 556) :

" Their Crowns send forth Rays. The Brilliancy of Their Bodies is as the Life of the Space into which They are come.

" The Word (Logos) that comes out of Their Mouth is Eternal Life ; and the Light that comes forth from Their Eyes is Rest for Them.

" The Movement of Their Hands is Their Flight to the Space out of which They are come ; and Their Gazing on Their own Faces is Gnosis of Themselves.

" The Going to Themselves is a repeated Return ; and the Stretching forth of Their Hands establishes Them.

" The Hearing of Their Ears is the Perception in Their Heart ; and the

46

Union of Their Limbs is the Ingathering of Israel.

"Their Holding to one another is Their Fortification in the Logos."

All this is doubtless "foolishness" to many but it is Light and Life and Wisdom for some few, who would strive towards becoming the Many in One, and One in Many.

But to the somewhat lesser mysteries of our ritual. All the terms must, I think, be interpreted as mystery-words; they contained for the Gnostics a wealth of meaning, which differed for each according to his understanding and experience. If, then, I venture on any suggestions of meaning, it should be understood that they are but tentative and ephemeral, and as it were only rough notes in pencil in the margin that may be rubbed out and emended by every one according to his knowledge and preference.

"I would be saved."

The human soul is "wandering in the

labyrinth of ills," as the Naassene Hymn
has it (*T.G.H.*, i. 191) ; is being swirled
about by the "fierce flood" of Ignorance
as the Preacher, in one of the Trismegistic
sermons, phrases it (*T.G.H.*, ii. 120).
The soul is being swirled about in the
Ocean of Genesis, in the Spheres of Fate.

She prays for safety, for that state of
stability which is attained when the worlds
of swirl in the Magna Vorago, or Great
Whirlpool, to use a term of the Orphic
tradition, are transcended, by means of
at-one-ment with the Great Stability, the
Logos—"He who stands, has stood and
will stand," as the Simonian *Great An-
nouncement* calls Him.

In its beginnings this safety expresses
neither motion nor stability, but a ceasing
from agitation ; the mind or anxiety is
no longer within the movement, the
Procession of Fate.

The tempest-tossed self cries out to be
drawn apart from the swirl ; while the
other self that is not in the swirl would
like to enter.

THE HYMN OF JESUS

The self within, or subject to, the
" downward " elements has to unite with
the self of the " upward " elements in
order to be saved from the swirling of the
passions ; while the " higher " self has to
be drawn into the " lower," so to say, and
unite with it, in order to be " saved "
from the incapacity of self-expression.

" I would be loosed."
That is, loosed from the bonds of Fate
and Genesis. In some of the rites the
candidate was bound with a rope. In
Egypt the rope symbolized a serpent, the
Typhonic " loud-breathing serpent " of
the passions, as the " Hymn of the Soul "
of Bardaisan calls it (*F.F.F.*, p. 477).

" I would be wounded."
Or " I would be pierced." This
suggests the entrance of the ray of the
higher self into the heart whereby the
" knot in the heart," as the Upaniṣhads
phrase it, may be unloosed, or dissolved,
or in order that the lower self may receive

the divine radiance of the higher. This
interpretation is borne out by the alternative reading from a Latin translation,
which may have originated in a gloss by
one who knew the mystery, for he writes :
" I would be dissolved " ; that is, " consumed by love."

And so we continue with the mysteries
of this truly " Sacred Marriage," or
" Spiritual Union," as it was called.

" I would be begotten."

This is the Mystery of the Immaculate
Conception, or Self-birth. " I would be
begotten " as a Christ, the New Man, or
True Man, who is in verity the Alone-
begotten—that is, Begotten-from-Himself-
alone, or Self-begotten.

" I would eat."

By " eating," food and eater become
one. The Logos is called the " Bread of
Life " ; that is, the Supersubstantial
Bread, one of the Elements of the Euchar-
ist. The soul desires to " eat " the Life

in everything ; this expresses how the
soul must become everything before it
can enjoy cosmic consciousness, and be
nourished by the Life in all.

So is it that men can become part of
the Cosmos through right action. But
to reach this consummation we must no
longer long to live and act our little life,
but rather to be, if one may so phrase it,
in our turn " eaten " ; that is to say, to
have our own self-will eaten out of us.
And then our fate or life or activity becomes part of the Great Records, and the
man becomes a Living Oracle or Drama, a
Christ. All Life then becomes a happen-
ing with meaning ; but this can never be
until the man surrenders his self-will and
becomes one with the Great Will.

This " eating " signifies a very intimate
kind of union, in which the life of a man
becomes part of a Great Life.

" I would hear."

It is to be remarked that there is no
" I would see." If we can legitimately

51

lay any stress on this, it is presumably
because the candidate is already "seeing";
he has already reached the "epopt"
stage, and therefore this "hearing" is
beyond the probationary stage of "hearing" or of the "mystēs."

Hearing is much more cosmic or
"greater" than seeing, as we learn later
on from our fragment, in the Vision of the
Cross, where John "sees the Lord Himself
above the Cross, not having any shape,
but only a voice."

In such hearing the hearer draws nigh
unto the Root-sound, or Breath (Ātman),
which creates all that it is possible to see.
To see there must be form, even if the
form is only an idea.

Again, hearing may be said to be the
verb of action when power is being con-
veyed to a person ; while seeing is the
verb of action of that person after re-
ceiving the power.

"I would understand."

This recalls the idea of "standing,"

" stability." Plato attributes this understanding to the Sphere of Sameness (the Eighth), in this, I believe, handing on an echo from Egypt. It is by means of this stability of the true mind that consciousness is enabled to link on the happenings in the whirling spheres, or whorls, of Fate to the Great Things or Things-that-are, and so perceive greater soul-records in phenomena. The last clause is evidently a gloss, but by a knowing scribe. The *Logos* is the *true* Understanding or Mind (*Nous*).

" I would be washed."

That is, I would be baptized, or immersed wholly in the Ocean of Living Water, the Great Oneness. It may mean simply " I would be purified." But the full rite of baptism was immersion and not sprinkling; as Thrice-greatest Hermes says in the sermon " The Cup," or " The Monad " (*T.G.H.*, ii. 86) :

" He filled a Mighty Cup (Kratēr) with

53

it (Mind), and sent it down, joining a
Herald to it, to whom He gave command
to make this proclamation to the hearts
of men :

" ' Baptize thyself with this Cup's baptism, what heart can do so, thou who
hast faith thou canst ascend to Him Who
hath sent down the Cup, thou who dost
know for what thou didst come into
being ! '

" As many then as understand the
Herald's tidings and *dowsed themselves* in
Mind, became partakers in the Gnosis ;
and when they had ' received the Mind '
they were made ' perfect men.' "

The Cup is perchance the Presence
substantially.

" Grace leadeth the dance."
In the text this has the next sentence
run on to it ; but I am myself inclined to
think that it is a note or a rubric rather

than an utterance of the Initiator.

The ceremony changes. Hitherto there had been the circle-dance, the "going round in a ring," which enclosed the mystery-drama, and the chanting of the sacred word.

Contact is now mystically established with the Great Sphere, Charis or Sophia, the Counterpart or Spouse or Syzygy of the Supernal Christ, or of the Christ Above. She "leads the dance"; that is to say, the actors begin to act according to the great cosmic movements.

"I would pipe."

In the Naassene Document (*T.G.H.*, i. 183), we read :

"The Phrygians also say that that which is generated from Him is Syriktēs."

Syriktēs is the Piper, properly the player on the syrinx, or seven-reeded Pan-pipe, whereby the music of the spheres is created.

And on this the early Jewish commentator remarks :

" For that which is generated is Spirit in harmony."

That is to say, Spirit, or Sophia the Holy Breath, is harmony ; and the Harmony was the name of the Seven Spheres encircled by the Eighth.   Curiously enough, later on in our fragment the Logos is called " Wisdom in harmony."

The Greek word for " dance " in the sentence " dance ye all " is different from that in the phrase " leadeth the dance." It reminds us of the " orchēstra " in the Greek theatre.

The Greek drama, I hold, arose from the Mysteries.   The general view, however, is that it " sprang from the choral dances round the altar of Dionysus," and so the architectural form of the Greek theatre " was developed from the circular dancing place," the *orchēstra*.

The dance is to represent the dance of

the world-mystery, and therefore of the
man-mystery—of joy and sorrow, of
rejoicing and beating the breast.

It is hardly necessary here to remind
the reader of the Gospel-saying taken by
the first (*Matth.*, xi. 17) and third (*Lk.*,
vii. 27) Evangelist from a common
source :

" We have piped unto you, and ye
have not danced ;
" We have played a dirge unto you, and
ye have not lamented."

Is it possible that there was an inner
tradition of a scripture in which this
Saying stood in the first person singular ?
I think I have made out a presumption
in my analysis of the Naassene Document
(*T.H.G.*, i. 195) that the Christian commentator, in his parallels with the Fourth
Gospel, legitimately opens up for us the
question whether or no he was in touch
with " sources " of that " Johannine "
document.

In any case, I would suggest that for the Gnostic there was an under-meaning, and that it is here in our Hymn expressed for us though still mystically hidden.

The higher quaternion, or tetrad, as the Gnostic Marcus would have phrased it, of joy is to blend with the lower tetrad of sorrow ; and both together are to form an octave, whereby the man is raised from his littleness into the Greatness ; that is to say, he can now respond to cosmic music.

Therefore what was apparently originally a rubric (" The one Eight " etc.), has been put by an unknowing scribe into the mouth of the Initiator, and an Amen added.

The Ogdoad or Eight (in music the full Octave), " sounds with us " ; that is, we are now beginning to dance to the Music of the Spheres.

And this being so, the sense of the initiated soul may be said to become cosmic, for it begins to vibrate with, or answer back to, or become in sympathy with, the ordered motions of the Greatness; and therefore the Higher Twelve, the Powers that transcend the separated soul, and which crown or surround the Great Sphere, now lead the dance.

Or, to speculate more daringly; the indications seem to denote a belief that at this stage in the rite there was present the Presence of Masterhood; and this would mean for the aspirant—as is so nobly set forth in the Trismegistic " Secret Sermon on the Mount," which might very well be called " The Initiation of Tat "— that he passes out of himself to greater things.

And so his " twelve disciples," as it were, begin to dance above him or outside him; for the real disciples or apostles of a new-born Christ are not the things he has been taught on earth as man, but powers raying forth from the true Person into still greater regions.

Apostles who go forth into the world of men are but reflections of Great Powers

who now go forth from the true Person
and link him on to the Great Cosmos.

It is not easy to conjecture the meaning
of the phrase " all whose nature is to
dance doth dance," for the text is
so faulty that we cannot be certain of a
correct version. If, however, this be the
right rendering, then I would suggest that
the " all " is the cosmic order ; and that
now all is made ready, and spiritual
communion has been established between
the church, or circle below, and the
Church Above, who again is the Supernal
Sophia.

" Who danceth not, knows not what is
being done."
The soul must dance, or be active in
a corresponding way, with the Great
Dance, in order to know, or attain true
Gnosis. Knowledge of the Great World
can only be attained when the man has
abandoned his self-will and acts in harmony with the Great Happenings.

This reminds us of the Saying in the Fourth Gospel (vii. 17) : " If a man will to do His Will, he shall know of the Doctrine " ; and again (ix. 31) : " If a man be a worshipper of God and do His Will, He will hear him." And the Will of God is His Divine Spouse, the Sophia or Wisdom, by Whom and in Whom He has made the worlds.

" I would flee."

It may be that here the new-born is in fear ; the new motions of the Great Passion are too great for him. Or, again, it may signify the necessity of balance, or equilibrium ; the soul feels itself swept away into the infinitudes, and is held back by the greater power of the Master —the that in him which alone is stable ; these two are then the centrifugal and centripetal powers.

" I would be adorned."

The original Greek term suggests the idea of being rightly "ordered" (*kosmein*).

It may also mean " clothed in fit gar-
ments " ; that is, the soul prays that his
little cosmos, which has previously been
awry or out of order, may be made like
unto the Great Order, and so he may be
clad in " glories " or " robes of glory "
or " power " like unto the Great Glories
of the Heavenly Spheres.

" I would be at-oned."
We now approach the mystery of
union, when the soul abandons with joy
its separateness, and frees itself from the
limitations of its " possessions "—of that
which is " mine " as apart from the rest.

And so we have the triple declaration
as to the loss of " dwelling," " place "
and " temple " (the very " shrine " of
the soul), and the assurance of the gain
of all " dwellings," " places " and
" temples." And in illustration of this
sublime idea we may yet again quote
from the " Untitled Apocalypse " of the
Bruce Codex (*F.F.F.*, p. 554) :

" ' Holy, Holy, Holy is He, the [here come the seven vowels each three times repeated] '

" That is to say :

" ' Thou art the Living One among the living.

" ' Thou art the Holy One among the holy.

" ' Thou art Being among beings.

" ' Thou art Father among fathers.

" ' Thou art God among gods.

" ' Thou art Lord among lords.

" ' Thou art Space among spaces.'

" Thus too do they praise Him :

" ' Thou art the House ;

" ' And Thou art the Dweller in the House.'

" And yet again do they praise the Son hidden in Him :

" ' Thou art ; Thou art the Alone-begotten—Light, Life and Grace.' "

" The Son of Man hath nowhere to lay His head " — for indeed He has all " places " in His possession.

Then follow the comfortable words that the Christ, the Logos, is the Lamp, the Mirror, the Door and the Way for the human soul; the Divine Soul is all things for the beloved.

In the worlds of darkness and uncertainty Christ is the Lamp, whom we must follow, for He leads us along the Way.

For those who can perceive the Christ-essence in all, this Christ-essence is a Mirror reflecting the great truths of the higher worlds.

There is one means alone of passing through the Wall of Separation between the Higher and the Lower, and that is Christ the Mediator. He is the Door; even as Thrice-greatest Hermes calls the Mind the "Inner Door" (*T.G.H.*, iii. 274). And Parmenides in his "Truthwards" refers to the same mystery when he describes the Gates, twixt Day and Night, or Light and Darkness.

For him who truly knocks at this Door,

that is who turns all his attention and power in this direction, the Great Wall or Limit will be no more, and he shall go in and out at will.

Again, Christ the Logos is the Way. He is our Path to God, both on the Light-side of things and on the Substance-side ; either as a Lamp, or that for which the pure mind looks, or a Way, that on which the feet walk. In either case the Christ is that which leads to God.

The ceremony again changes with the words : " Now answer to My dancing."

All now may be believed to be taking place within the Master-Presence. Union of substance has been attained, but not yet union of consciousness. Before that final mystery can be consummated, the knowledge of the Passion of Man, that is of the Great Passion or perpetual experience of the Great Act, must be achieved.

The soul is to gaze upon the mystery as upon its own Passion. The perfected soul can gaze upon the mystery in peace; as yet, however, the soul of the aspirant is not perfected in gnosis, but in substance only, so that it may feel the Great Passion in itself, and yet as apart from itself.

Hereupon in the lower rite, the mystery-drama, the Passion of Man, must have been shown. What it may have been is not easy to conjecture; it must, however, have been something of a most distressing nature, for the neophyte is moved or shaken completely—that is to say, un-nerved. He had not the strength of perfect faith in the Power of the Master; for, presumably, he saw that very Master dismembered before his eyes, or becoming many from one, or in some way done to death.

After the Passion-drama or Passion-vision comes the instruction; for in such rites—such passions or experiences for the sake of knowing—there must be the actual experience in feeling before there can be gnosis.

This knowledge is given by the Master Himself, the Logos in man : Wherefore it needs must be the lover should first behold the Beloved suffering.

And then follow the comfortable words : " I am a couch ; rest thou upon Me." For the Suffering Christ is but the translation into manifestation in time and space of the Triumphant Eternal Christ, the Æon. It is here that that mystery of Docetism, of what the Vedānta calls Māyā, receives a philosophical meaning. This mystery is suggested in many a *logos* ; but here I will quote only from the Trismegistic sermon called " The Inner Door " (*T.G.H.*, iii. 275) :

" And being so minded and so ordering his life, he shall behold the Son of God becoming all things for holy souls, that he may draw her (the soul) forth from out the region of the Fate into the Incorporeal.

" For having power in all, He becometh all things, whatsoever He will; and in obedience to the Father's nod, through the whole Body doth He penetrate, and pouring forth His Light into the mind of every soul, He starts it back into the Blessed Region, where it was before it had become corporeal—following after Him, and led by Him into the Light."

" Who I am thou shalt know when I depart."

This and the two following sentences seem to suggest—that is, if we may venture to believe that there was true vision of an inner mystery accompanying the outer drama—some such idea as this.

The substantial nature of the Presence, the Body, so to speak, of atmosphere, which may have been seen—with some suggestion of an idea of human form as its " pillar " or " support," and at the same time of a sphere or completeness

holding it together—this, says the Master,
is not my true Self. I am not this Mirror
of the World, I am not this Word or
Living Symbol which contains the whole
world, and also stamps it with meaning
and idea. What the nature of the real
Christ is thou shalt know when thou
comest, or becomest Him.

" If thou hadst known how to
suffer."

The sentences so beginning are perhaps
the most pregnant in meaning in the
whole of this marvellous ritual. It seems
in one sense (for there are infinite meanings) to signify : If the substance of your
body had really known how to dance, and
so been able to respond exactly to My Passion (that is, the manifestation in activity
of real life and consciousness), then you
would have had the power to have kept
stable about the Mystic Centre, and not
have been dragged back into your body
of suffering, or in-harmony ; you would
not have been dragged back onto the

dramatic side of things and been swamped by the drama.

"That which thou knowest not, I Myself will teach thee."

That which the soul unaided cannot know, the Master will teach. That is to say, presumably: This Power or Presence is a link between your own "body" or atmosphere and the realities of Great Things.

As soon as the sphere-"body" (the psychic envelope of normal man is said to be an ellipse, egg-shaped, imperfect) is capable of dancing, the Power of the Master will stamp it with meaning. The little self cannot do this. The Power is not connected with little things. It comes from the greater worlds as a natural result of the perfect dancing of the substances of all man's "bodies."

"I am thy God, not the Betrayer's."
Taken in connection with the introductory words before our Hymn, this will probably

suggest to most readers the thought of Judas. But the Gnostics moved in a wider circle of ideas.

The Betrayer is rather the lawless Serpent, the Kakodaimōn, that which hands the soul over to the bodies of death—a mystery that is not touched upon in our ritual.

" I would be kept in time with holy souls."

This sentence appears to me to be misplaced. One of its meanings seems to be that as the soul watches the Dance, it prays to be brought into harmony with " Holy Souls " ; that is to have its consciousness and form brought into such perfect relationship as to become one. Then the little soul would become a Great Soul or Master, a Perfect or Balanced Soul.

The concluding sentences are evidently drawn from two different traditions of the original text ; they are two separate

endings copied down one after the other.
It is thus to be conjectured that there
were several variants of this ritual, and
that it was, therefore, widely known and
used in Gnostic circles.

It must, however, have been at first
kept very secret, for later on in the text
of our fragment we read the injunction
of the Master to John :

" That Passion which I showed unto
thee and unto the rest in the Dance, I
will that it be called a mystery."

Can it be that in the original form, it
was John, the Beloved himself, who was
the candidate ?

It may have been so ; but even if so,
" John " would not be understood by a
Gnostic to be the name of one single
historical character. There had been,
there were, and there would be many
Johns.

From the Twelve Three; and from the
Three One.

For just as we find that there were Three—Peter, James and John—who were nearest the Lord in His Great Moments, so also do we find in the Johannine tradition that of these Three, it was John who was nearest to Him in His Great Acts.

Moreover, just as in the Trismegistic tradition we find that out of the Three— Ammon, Asclepius and Tat—it is Tat, the most spiritual of the disciples, who succeeds his " Father," Thrice-greatest Hermes, when He is taken to the Gods ; so also do we find in the Johannine tradition that it is John who succeeds Jesus when He ascends to the Father of all " Fathers."

" Father " was the technical name of the Master, or Initiator, and the Head of the community.

And so, in a codex of the Fourth Gospel, preserved in the archives of the Templars of St. John of Jerusalem, in Paris—that is to say in all probability in a document that belonged to those who came into contact with the Johannine tradition in the East—we find (Thilo, *Cod. Apoc. N.T.*, p. 880) the following additions which are absent from the Textus Receptus.

To *John*, xvii. 26 :

" Amen, I say unto you, I am not of this world ; but John shall be your Father, till he shall go with Me into Paradise. And He anointed them with the Holy Spirit."

And to *John*, xix. 26-30 :

" He saith to His Mother : Weep not ; I go to My Father and to Eternal Life. Behold Thy Son. He will keep My place.

" Then saith He to the Disciple : Behold thy Mother !

" Then bowing His Head He breathed forth His Spirit."

But if it be willed that that which " I showed unto thee . . . in the Dance" be " called a mystery," it must equally be willed that it be kept a mystery.

I therefore offer my surmises on the altar of the Outer Court, though hardly venturing to think they will be regarded as reasonable oblations to the Great Presence by many of the Many who serve there.

I would, however, venture to hope that I have at least established a strong presumption that the Hymn of Jesus is no hymn, but a very early Christian mystery-ritual, and perhaps the oldest Christian ritual of any kind preserved to us.

BIBLIOGRAPHY.

LIPSIUS (R. A.), *Die apocryphen Apostelgeschichten* (Braunschweig, 1883).

CORSSEN (P.), *Monarchianische Prologe zu den Vier Evangelien, T. u. A.*, xv. i. (Leipzig, 1896).

JAMES (M. R.), *Apocrypha Anecdota, T. and S.*, v. i. (Cambridge, 1897).

BONNET (M.), *Acta Apostolorum Apocrypha* (Leipzig, 1898).

HENNECKE (E.), *Neutestamentliche Apokryphen* (Tübingen, 1904).

MEAD (G. R. S.), *Fragments of a Faith Forgotten*, 2nd. ed. (London, 1906).

MEAD (G. R. S.), *Thrice Greatest Hermes* (London, 1906).

OTHER QUEST BOOK MINIATURE TITLES

The Voice of the Silence
At the Feet of the Master
The Sayings of the Ancient One
Light on the Path
The Song Celestial
The Buddhist Catechism
Tao—a Poetic Version
Thoughts for Aspirants

For a complete descriptive list of all
Quest Books write to:

QUEST BOOKS
P.O. Box 270, Wheaton, Ill. 60187